THE WORLD OF SKATEBOARDING

A BEGINNER'S GUIDE TO VERY COOL SKATEBOARDING TRICKS

Aaron Rosenberg

the rosen publishing group's

rosen central

Published in 2003 by The Rosen Publishing Group
29 East 21st Street, New York, NY 10010

Library of Congress Cataloging-in-Publication Data

Rosenberg, Aaron.
A beginner's guide to very cool skateboarding tricks / Aaron Rosenberg.
    p. cm. — (The world of skateboarding)
Includes bibliographical references (p.) and index.
Summary: Discusses skateboard basics, offering tips on buying a skateboard,
maintenance, safety gear, terminology, and step-by-step instructions for more
than ten tricks.
ISBN 0-8239-3646-5 (lib. bdg.)
1. Skateboarding—Juvenile literature. [1. Skateboarding.
2. Skateboards.]
I. Title. II. Series.
GV859.8 .R67 2003
796.22—dc21

2001007616

Manufactured in the United States of America

CONTENTS

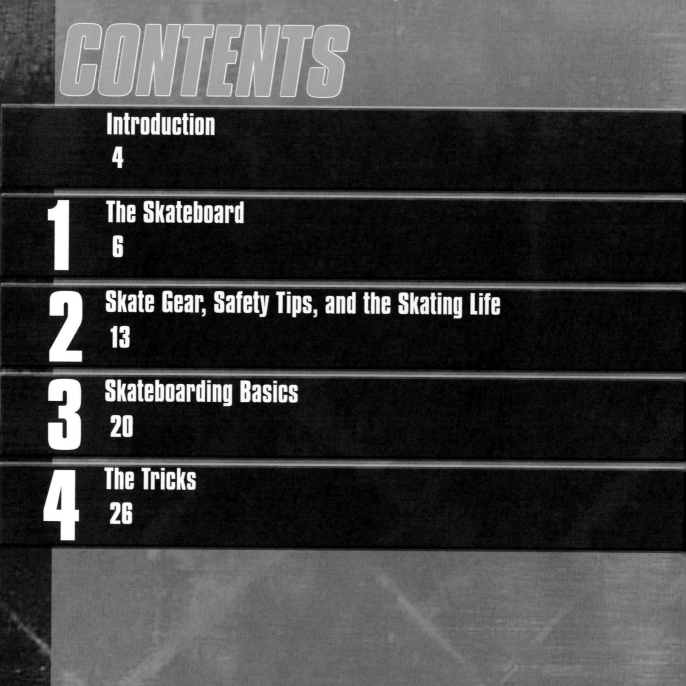

INTRODUCTION

So you want to skateboard. Great! This book will help you get started. You'll learn all the tricks that a beginning skater needs to know. These are the tricks that pros invented. You'll learn about skateboards and how to choose the right one for yourself. You'll also learn about skating gear and safety tips. Everything you need to get you on your board and on the road is right here!

So why skateboard anyway? There are a lot of reasons. First of all, it's fun. Skateboarding gives you a great sense of freedom: riding your board, feeling the ground race beneath your feet and the wind whip through your hair, the sense of control as you spin and flip and twist. The skateboard experience is exhilarating.

Skateboarding is also a way to express yourself. No two people do tricks exactly the same. The way you combine tricks and even the way you ride says something about who you really are. It's also a good way to meet people your own age who have a common interest.

Skateboarding is good exercise, too. But it's exercise that's fun to do. It doesn't require a lot of heavy or expensive equipment. You

Skateboarding is a great way to pass the time with friends, exercise your body, meet new people, and have fun.

can skateboard by yourself, or hook up with other skaters. And if you practice your tricks, you'll not only get noticeably better, you'll win the admiration of friends and strangers alike. All in all, it's a great sport—and with practice maybe you can become a pro skater yourself.

The skateboard is your tool, your transport, and your instrument. Getting to know your skateboard gives you a quick understanding of its dynamics. Knowing what each part does helps you learn tricks.

THE NUTS AND BOLTS OF A SKATEBOARD

Skateboards are made up of lots of little parts, but there are five major elements to every board:

The Deck

The deck is the actual wooden board, the part you stand on. It's the single largest piece of any skateboard. Decks are usually laminated plywood (thin layers of wood glued together for increased strength and flexibility). Skateboard decks vary in size, shape, and length. Most decks have a raised tail and nose.

Grip Tape

Grip tape covers the top of the deck. It feels like coarse sandpaper and gives your shoes grip as you skate. Grip tape is helpful for tricks because you need extra "stick" to move the board around.

Trucks

Trucks connect the wheels to the deck. Each board has two trucks, front and back. The trucks control how well the board turns, both the angle and the speed. Trucks can be adjusted, made tighter or looser. Each skater has a preference.

Wheels

There are four wheels on a board—two in front and two in back. Today, skateboard wheels are made of urethane (synthetic rubber) compounds. They're built to absorb shocks, to grip the road well, and to last. Wheels are designed for specific terrain: Wheels made for the street won't work well on ramps, and vice versa. Street wheels are usually softer so the ride won't feel so rough; ramp wheels are harder to help you go faster.

Bearings

The bearing is a set of eight small ball bearings (metal balls) placed within a small ring. Each wheel also has two precision bearings (separated by a washer, or bearing spacer), connecting the wheel to the axle (on the truck). The bearings help the wheels turn smoothly. They also stabilize each wheel as it spins on the axle.

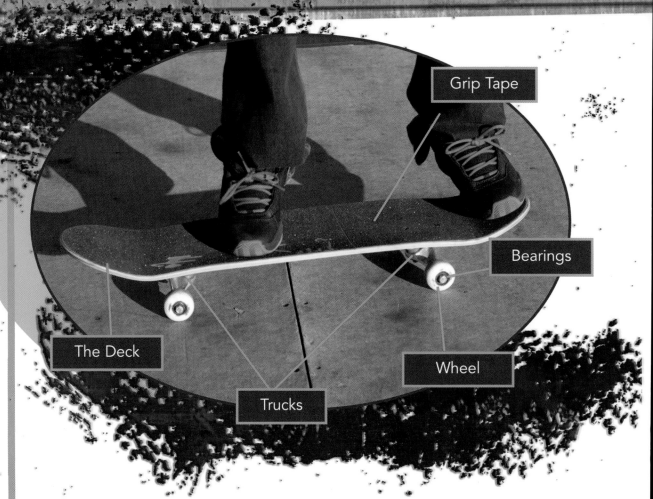

Grip Tape

Bearings

The Deck

Wheel

Trucks

CHOOSING A SKATEBOARD

You're about to buy your first skateboard. Which is best for you?

First, consider buying a used skateboard since they cost less. You should at least try out a couple of used skateboards to get an idea of how different boards ride. New boards, of course, have no wear and tear on them. All their parts are tightly attached and ready for some hard riding. There really isn't much difference in the quality of the brands. Owning one or the other is a matter of preference. It's more important to choose a board that feels right in size and shape.

Skateboard Sizes

Your skateboard needs to be small enough and light enough for you to control easily. Likewise, it must be large enough to handle the size of your feet and your weight. Skateboard decks are classified in two lengths: traditional/street (under thirty-three inches) and longboard (over thirty-five inches).

Traditional decks work better for doing tricks. They give you the best control. Longboards are used more if you're just going to ride and glide. Traditional decks vary in width, though usually they're between seven and eight-and-a-half inches wide.

How Skateboards Are Made

Modern skateboards are most often made from a wood multi-ply. The standard is seven plies of sugar maple veneer glued together using polyvinyl glues. The plies are placed in a press and squeezed together while the glue dries. The boards are removed from the press and shaped into the proper curve.

After days of curing (when the wood dries and fixes into the curve) a deck template is used to trace the shape and size of the finished deck. A band saw makes the rough cuts. The final shape is made using sanders and files. A wood sealer protects the deck from moisture. After that, it's just a matter of painting the board and affixing the trucks and wheels.

Look for a board big enough to fit your feet. You can measure the proper board length for your size by putting one foot in front of the other, heel to toe. The length of the board should be equal to or greater than the length of your feet. Also, the board width should allow your feet, when placed side by side, to fit entirely. If both rules are met, you've found the right size board. Your weight shouldn't be an issue, but your height is. The smaller you are, the more likely you'll want a smaller board because it's easier to control.

Flexibility

Your board should be stiff enough to support your weight without bending more than an inch in the middle. The board should have some flex in it, though. A board that is too stiff will break more easily. If it's too flexible, it will sag. That means you'll have a hard time keeping your footing.

Checking for Wear

Most new skateboards come with grip tape already on the deck. If you're buying a used board, though, the grip tape might be worn out. You'll need good grip tape to do most tricks. Also, check used boards for chips in the deck. Too many chips might mean the board is about worn out. If this is the case, look for another one.

Be sure to also check the trucks on the board. They should be tightly attached, both to the board and to the wheels. Some scrapes and nicks are O.K., but they shouldn't be too battered. Push the board around to make sure the trucks and wheels are on properly—and that they work. Try turning. Good trucks let you make tight turns.

Skateboard Maintenance

Skateboards are like any other vehicle: You need to take good care of them if they're to last. If you take a few minutes before each session to check over your board, it will work better and you'll have a cleaner, safer ride. Here are a few things to watch for:

Decks: Check for cracks. Minor cracks appear from normal use. If the cracks go through several layers of wood, or if the top layer is starting to peel up, you need a new deck.

Grip tape: Dirty grip tape won't give you good traction. Take a little water and a plastic bristle brush and clean the tape. Let the board dry in the sun.

Truck mounting hardware: This is what holds the trucks to the deck. Check to make sure they're tight. Don't overtighten the bolts.

Trucks: Check the rubber pieces (bushings and pivot caps) to make sure they haven't been crushed. Check the metal (hangers and base plates) for any cracks. You can buy replacement parts for minor repairs.

Axle wheel lock nuts: These hold your wheels onto the trucks. Always check these before skateboarding. It's a good idea to check them during sessions as well. The nuts can loosen over time. If the nut doesn't tighten or stay tight, replace it.

Wheels: Look for large chunks of missing urethane, deep grooves and scratches, or flat spots.

Bearings: If your wheels aren't spinning smoothly, or if they make noise, you may need to clean the bearings. Some bearings don't come apart and need to be replaced when they wear down. If the bearings do come apart, you can take them out, spray them with a little solvent, add some lubricant, and then put them back together. To prevent wear and tear it's best to buy sealed bearings. They keep dirt and moisture out, which will save you the trouble of having to clean them.

You need to check every part of a used skateboard before you buy one, especially the trucks.

Think about the size of your wheels. Larger wheels take longer to get up to speed, but they give you more control when going fast. Small wheels let you turn quicker but with less control. Smaller wheels are also lighter and allow you to do tricks more easily. As a rule of thumb, smaller wheels are designed for street skating while larger wheels are better suited for the ramps. As you see, the proper wheel setup is important to where and how you ride.

Finally, check to see that the wheels spin freely. If they resist, or start and stop, you may only need to loosen the bolts that keep the wheels on the trucks. If that doesn't help, you may need new bearings.

It's best not to just buy a skateboard and hop on. You must think about skate safety when beginning this sport. Skateboard champions like Tony Hawk have always worn helmets, and elbow and knee pads. You *will* be falling in this sport, and you need to take precautions.

SAFETY GEAR

The safety gear basics you'll need are a helmet, knee pads, wristguards, and elbow pads. Make sure to get either Consumer Product Safety Commission (CPSC)–approved gear or European CE–approved gear. Both regulate safety standards on many products and sports equipment used in the United States, Canada, and Europe.

Helmet

Your helmet is the single most important safety item you can wear when skating. Helmets come in lots of colors and a variety of shapes, but there are two different helmet designs. The first is built to protect you from minor bangs and scrapes. The other is designed to handle more serious impacts. CPSC-approved helmets are the latter type. They can withstand minor scrapes as well, but will also protect you in a major collision. Make sure your helmet fits properly. It shouldn't be too tight, but it also shouldn't slip when you shake your head.

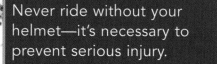

Never ride without your helmet—it's necessary to prevent serious injury.

Skateboarding helmets and bicycle helmets are interchangeable. They use the same safety standards. Always wear your helmet, because the first time you land on your head you'll be glad you have that protection.

Wrist Guards

When you fall, the first thing you do is put your hands out. Your instincts force you to react this way. Wrist guards wrap around your palms and ride up your forearms. They protect you from scrapes, hard-impact falls, and overbending your wrists.

Knee Pads

The knee is one of the most vulnerable parts of your body. It gets damaged easily and heals slowly. As a skateboarder you'll be using your knees a lot. Knee pads will keep your knees safe from scrapes and hard-impact falls.

Make sure the pads you buy have a hard plastic cap. Hard plastic caps absorb more impact. They also slide over the ground when you fall. This keeps your knee from twisting on the ground. Make sure the pads are tight enough to stay in place, but loose enough that they don't restrict movement or cut off circulation.

Good elbow pads should fit securely so they can withstand the impact of your fall.

Elbow Pads

Elbows don't get hit as often as knees, but they do get scraped. A good set of elbow pads should fit nice and snug. They shouldn't come off when you hit the ground. Look for elbow pads that have hard plastic caps.

Gloves

You don't need gloves all the time, but for some tricks you might want them. If you're skateboarding on gravel, gloves are a good idea. Otherwise you can scrape your hands when you fall. Go for full-finger gloves unless you know your fingers aren't at risk. And if you're doing a lot of tricks where your hands could get hurt, buy heavier gloves with padding sewn in.

Shoes

Special shoes are required for skateboarding. While you can wear your average tennis or basketball shoes on the board, they will get torn up very quickly. A shoe specific to skateboarding usually has rubber padding on the outside curve to protect against the grip tape when doing tricks. This is the section of the shoe that takes the most abuse. Airwalk and Vans shoes are among the most popular and respected brands among the pros.

SKATEBOARDING SAFETY TIPS

Since you're going to fall on a regular basis while skating, it helps to know how to fall properly. Here are some tips on how to fall that will prevent injury:

- When you lose your balance, crouch down a bit. If you do end up falling you'll have a shorter distance between you and the ground.

- Remember to land on the more fleshy parts of your body. The butt is ideal, but your stomach and chest are also good. You do not want to land on your head, elbows, hips, or knees.

- Our natural reaction when we fall is to catch ourselves with our hands and arms. Don't do this! You're likely to break a bone as your weight hits. Instead, roll into a ball and roll with the fall. Your impact is spread out more evenly, and you roll instead of scraping along the ground.

- Try to relax. If your body is loose instead of stiff, you can roll more easily and have a better chance of avoiding injury.

THE SKATING LIFE: WHERE CAN I SKATE?

So now you have a board and safety gear. You're ready to start skating! But where do you go?

Skateboarding can be done on many surfaces. When you're starting out, though, you want a nice flat surface without a lot of bumps. An empty garage is an ideal starting place—it gives you a nice smooth surface and enough room to move, but no obstacles to hit, trip over, or hurt yourself on. Driveways also work well, too, as long as they're not full of cracks and there aren't any cars in the way. Once you've gotten the feel for the board, you can venture out a bit more.

Playgrounds are also good for skating, as are sidewalks. But you also need to know the rules. Some cities don't allow skateboarding on the sidewalks because it's too dangerous for people walking by. Check with your local police department to find out where you're allowed to skate. Many cities have skateparks specifically for skaters. Not only is the surface smooth and the area safe, but you can meet other skateboarders and

Skateboard Terms

Skateboarders have their own language to describe what they do. You need to learn it or suffer some good-natured teasing from your friends. Most terms describe obstacles or surfaces. Here are some basic terms to get you started in the skateboarding world. For more skating terms, check the glossary in the back of this book.

Bail
There are two meanings for bail: 1. to fall; 2. deciding in midair that you're not going to land your trick and kicking your board away for a painless landing.

Bank
Any incline used for riding up, completing a trick, and riding back down.

Coping
Any grindable and slidable material attached to an obstacle for easier grinds and slides.

Grind
Any variety of tricks where one or more truck hangers grind along the edge of an obstacle.

Ledge
Any raised surface used for grinding and sliding.

Lip
The edge of any obstacle that a skateboarder rides; on ramps, the lip usually is completed with coping; on a bank or curb, the square or angled corner is the lip.

Nose
The front end of the deck, before the first two mounting holes.

Pop
1. The amount of snap and stiffness to a board; 2. to smack the tail against the ground to begin a trick.

Session
Any time a group of skaters gets together at a spot.

Slide
Any variety of tricks where the board (but not the trucks) slides along coping, ledge, or lip.

Spot
Any place that has anything to skate.

Stick
To land a trick solid and clean.

Switch
Standing on the board in the opposite direction of your normal stance.

Tail
The back part of the deck, behind the last two mounting holes.

learn more about your board and how to use it. Skateparks are a great place to watch more seasoned skaters who can show you how tricks are done. Whatever you do, do not skateboard on the streets. This is highly dangerous. Cars and other vehicles may not see you in time to stop.

3 SKATEBOARDING BASICS

Now you've got your board and your gear, and you know some skate lingo. It's time to learn how to skate!

One thing to remember is that skateboarding is not as easy as it might look. Learning to skate well takes time and practice. Don't get upset and give up if you aren't doing tricks after your first day. Some people take weeks or months to master the simplest trick. Just remember—have fun as you learn how to skate.

Skateboarding is a sport, and it's physically demanding. When you're skating, you'll use your legs and feet the most. Your back and arms will also get worked out from stances and grabs. If you find the tricks difficult to start, or your body aches after a session, it's just because you're not yet used to the physical demands of skating. In time, you'll build muscle. If you stretch before and after a session, you're limbs will become more flexible, too. One of the reasons why skateboarding is so popular is that it provides a fun way to exercise.

We'll start small, then work our way up. Before you can start jumping obstacles and grinding down rails, you need to be able to stay on your board and skate along a flat surface.

STANCE

The first thing you have to work on is your stance. Learning to stand correctly on your skateboard is important for riding and doing tricks. Skateboarders refer to stances (and themselves) as being either regular-footed or goofy-footed. They are a skater's natural stance. Regular-footed is riding on the skateboard with your left foot forward, the way Andy McDonald rides. Goofy-footed is riding with your right foot forward, the way Tony Hawk rides. Keep in mind that neither stance is considered wrong or better than the other. What matters is which feels more comfortable.

When you step on a skateboard, does it feel better with your right foot forward or your left? Try it both ways to see which feels more natural. Once you've determined which is best for you, practice skating that way. Later, you can also try skating with your feet the opposite way (so if you're goofy-footed you could try with your left foot in front). This is called "switch" stance. You usually only switch to perform a trick that's easier the opposite way.

There are two common stances, one with the right foot forward, called goofy-footed *(left)*, and the other with the left foot forward, called regular-footed *(right)*.

Once you've got your footing, practice standing and balancing on the board. Keep both feet turned to the side. Space your feet apart so that they're over the trucks. The trucks are where you usually want your feet, because that's the sturdiest part of the board. Keeping your feet within a few inches to either side of each truck is fine. Try not to bring both feet to the center of the board; your weight may crack it. Now bend your knees a little for balance. Just get used to being on the board and balancing on it.

PUSHING OFF

Once you have your balance, you need to learn how to push off so that the skateboard is moving. Find some flat ground and start moving by pushing off slowly with one of your feet. This is usually done with your back foot (pushing off with your front foot is called pushing "mongo").

When pushing off, be sure to stay centered on the board. Shift forward so your weight is still on the board to prevent the board from shooting out from under you. To stop when you're going slow, step off the board with your back foot. Most skaters learn to drag the toe of their back foot to slow down when going fast.

Pushing off takes practice to maintain balance. Take a couple of pushes and stand on the board. Feel the speed and how your weight balances. Now it's time to turn.

You can steer your board in different directions by shifting your body weight.

STEERING

Once you're comfortable with starting and stopping your board, you're ready for the next step: steering. Steering is all about shifting your weight to one side or the other. The trucks move with the shifting board and steer the wheels in that direction.

Find a wide-open flat surface. Push off a few times and then stand on your board. Now you're moving forward. Shift your weight by bending your knees and using your ankles. Don't lean over one side or the other. This will throw off your balance. Weight shifting is all about using your legs and ankles along with your upper body to control your balance.

Let yourself turn slowly to the right or left. Now bring your weight back on top of the board. Now shift your weight to the other side. Steering is as easy as that. As you practice steering, you'll find that foot position on the board will help you turn tighter. Bending your knees further will also help maintain balance. Practicing your turns is key to understanding the dynamics of any skateboard.

You may find it easier to turn one way than the other. This direction is usually the opposite of your natural stance (goofy- or regular-footed). This isn't unusual. With practice you'll easily master the balance and weight distribution that control steering.

TIC TAC

Now that you can push off, turn, and ride at a moderate speed, it's time to learn your first trick! The tic tac is a simple trick that will show you how to move the nose of your board back and forth in a zigzag pattern.

Push off and move forward at a slow speed. Shift your weight to the tail and lift the nose in the air. As the nose is in the air, pivot back and forth using your back foot. Use your front foot to

The tic tac: 1. Push off and build up some speed.
2. Move your weight to the back, let the nose rise, and use your front foot to direct the nose of the board.
3. Repeat step 2, again changing directions.

direct the nose. To make the tic tac work best you have to balance on the back wheels while you're moving the nose.

You can tic tac to pick up more speed. You can also tic tac to keep your balance because it gives you a second to shift your weight and move your front foot slightly. Perfecting the tic tac is a good start to learning rear-wheel balance and balance recovery. Once you feel comfortable tic tac-ing, its time to move on to more tricks.

Now that you've got the basics, you can skateboard up and down the street and even around simple obstacles. But that isn't enough, is it? You want to learn some tricks. So here we go!

OLLIE

This is the most common trick for any skateboarder. The ollie is also used in a lot of harder tricks. Learning the ollie can be difficult at first, so make sure you have the basics down beforehand. This goes for each of the tricks in this book. To best perform the trick, understand the basics. Once you have the basics, it's just a matter of practice. Before attempting the ollie (or any trick), try to watch someone do it first. Seeing the ollie done gives you the right idea for the trick's beginning, middle, and end. You understand where your feet should be, how to move your feet and body, and how to land. Ready? Let's give it a try!

1 Try your first ollie with the board in one place. Stand on your board with your back foot on the tail and your front foot in the middle. (Your front foot should be closer than normal to your back foot). Slam the tail on the pavement.

2 At the same time, jump, lifting your front foot as high as you can. The front will pop up, and then the back will come off the ground. If you did it correctly, all four wheels will be in the air for an instant.

3 Once in the air, level the board out by moving your front foot forward and your back foot up to the same level as your front foot. This will make your ollie higher.

4 Land with your feet solidly over the trucks. If your feet are on the front and back, or are both in the center, you could break the board.

NOLLIE (NOSE OLLIE)

The nollie is an ollie using the nose of the board instead of the tail; it's an ollie in reverse. The hard part about the nollie is that you can't see your back foot moving. You have to learn to feel the board, and when to shift your weight around. For example, if you are goofy-footed, doing a nollie is like doing an ollie in the regular-footed position while going backward. Once you get it down, you'll be able to pop your board both backward and forward! You should learn the ollie well before attempting the nollie.

1 Place your front foot comfortably on the nose and your back foot over the middle of the board. Push down on the nose to get the best pop; the harder you push, the higher you go.

Slide your back foot toward the tail to help the board come off the ground.

3 When you feel like you have reached maximum height, your board should be level to the ground. Get your feet over the trucks. Now wait until you hit the ground, and roll away smoothly.

Ollie Grab

Before you take this trick to a ramp you should do it standing still. All you're doing with the ollie grab is grabbing the board in mid-ollie (while you're in the air). The hard part is that you have to ollie higher than normal in order to reach the board. You can grab any part of the board with either hand; it doesn't matter.

1 Stand on the board with your feet in ollieing position. Slam down on the tail and ollie. (When you first do this trick, just tap the board with your hand until you're comfortable with the maneuver.)

When your feet come up level to the board, reach down and grab the board. Remember to keep both feet in contact with the board while grabbing, and when you've finished the grab keep the board stuck to your feet. **2**

3 Let go of the board, extend your legs (straighten up), land, and roll away.

There are different names for the ollie grab depending on where and how you grab the board:

- Grabbing "mute" is grabbing the upper section of the board on your facing side, near the toes of your front foot.

- Grabbing "indy" is grabbing the back section on your facing side, near the toes of your back foot.

- Grabbing "backside" is grabbing the upper section on your back side, near the heel of your front foot.

- Grabbing "stalefish" is grabbing the lower section near the heel of your back foot.

FRONTSIDE 180 OLLIE

Frontside is a way of turning while doing a trick. A frontside ollie is when you turn in mid-ollie in the direction of your back. For example, if you skate regular-footed (your left foot being in front) you would turn left. If you skate goofy-footed, you would turn right. Once you can nail the ollie, try this hot trick.

If you do the frontside 180 correctly you'll land riding fakie, or backwards. Common problems people have while learning this trick include not being able to turn the complete 180 before landing. Another problem is an inability to land with both feet on the deck. The important thing to remember is that both feet play an equal role in moving the board. If you're having trouble, watch people who can frontside 180, and keep practicing.

Move along at a moderate speed, with your feet set to ollie. Snap down on your tail, and slide your front foot forward toward the nose.

As you go up into the ollie, twist your body frontside until you turn a complete half-circle—move your back foot around as far as you can and drag your front foot up and around the opposite way.

Keep both feet on the board at all times. Stay centered on your board and land on the trucks.

BACKSIDE 180 OLLIE

The backside 180 ollie works like the frontside 180, except you turn your body in the opposite direction, backside. This trick is a little easier than the frontside 180 since it's easier to leverage your body in the backside direction. Therefore, you might want to learn this trick before you learn frontside. Use caution, however, as this trick is hard to do while standing still or going slow.

Backside 180 Ollie

1 Roll forward at a moderate speed. As you ollie, sweep the board as well as your body in the backside direction.

Use both your feet to work together in rotating the board so that it lines up properly.

2

3 Come down with your feet over the trucks. Land and roll away. You should now be riding fakie, which is riding backward.

The trick is to keep your back foot on the board while rotating. Some skaters do this trick by doing their ollie at an angle. Others like to ollie first and begin to turn while they're in midair. This technique is better when you're trying to 180 ollie over a high object. The trick is to clear the object first and then turn your body.

POP SHOVE IT

The pop shove it is basically a 180 ollie without turning your body; only the board turns. You should learn the backside version of this trick first since it's easier.

The hardest part of the pop shove it is the landing. You want to time your landing just as the board completes its rotation. The frontside version of this trick is more difficult since it's harder to spin your legs in the frontside direction. The basics of the trick, however, are the same.

1 Begin as you would doing a backside 180 ollie. As the tail touches the ground, sweep both feet so the board spins in the backside direction. You don't have to ollie high, just enough so that the wheels clear the ground.

2 The board should spin horizontally as it lifts off the ground.

3 Land as the board completes its rotation. For the best results, try to land with both feet planted over the trucks.

KICKFLIP

The kickflip is one of the most popular skateboarding tricks today. Before learning the kickflip, you should be comfortable with the ollie, since this trick starts out the same way.

If you can ollie, pop shove it, and kickflip, you can learn most other skateboarding tricks, and even invent your own combinations.

Set your feet in an ollie position, but leave the heel of your front foot hanging off the edge of your board. Start an ollie. When in the air, push down on the edge of the board with the tip of your front foot. This should flip the board.

Let your legs stay above the board, and keep your weight centered.

When the board flips back over, catch it with your feet (press down just enough to keep it in place). Now land on the trucks.

BACKSIDE 180 KICKFLIP

The backside 180 kickflip is more difficult than the other tricks in this book. In order to learn it, you must know how to backside 180 ollie and how to kickflip. Make sure you can do both of these tricks well on their own.

1 Begin a backside 180 ollie, but ollie somewhat higher than normal.

The flip begins once you're in the air. Do a kickflip as your body is turning. (Note: Do not sweep the board with your feet as you would in a kickflip. You want to make sure that the board is turning at the same rate as your body.)

2

3 Set your feet above the trucks as the board completes its rotation.

Land smoothly on the trucks and ride away.

4

Then try doing them back to back to back—a backside 180 ollie, then a kickflip, then another backside 180 ollie. Hitting these back to back tells you that you can handle both halves of the trick, and even do them in rapid succession. The backside 180 kickflip also requires you to ollie a little higher than you would normally.

50–50 GRIND

The 50–50 is usually the first grind, or sliding on the trucks, that skateboarders learn. It involves sticking both trucks to a ledge, coping, or rail, and grinding along. When you lose speed, you hop off and ride away.

Before you grind, make sure the coping is grindable. In other words, make sure the coping is smooth enough for the trucks to slide. Test the curb out first by scraping the trucks along the coping. If the trucks slide easily, you're set. If they don't, find coping that's smoother. A painted curb is usually perfect for grinding. The paint smooths the surface. Unpainted curbs are usually too rough. Use your better judgment.

These instructions are for your standard ledge and coping. If you're going for a rail, just let the momentum of the ollie carry you forward or backward.

Another thing to keep in mind for grinds is that you should always have speed and confidence. The easiest way to get hurt on a grind is to go too slowly and stall out.

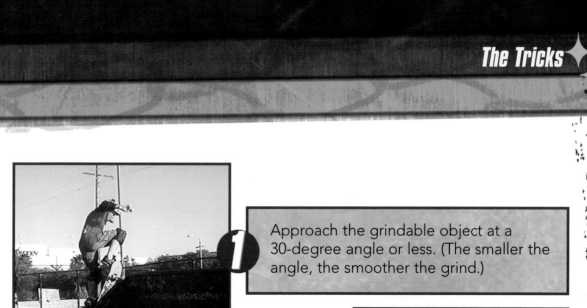

1 Approach the grindable object at a 30-degree angle or less. (The smaller the angle, the smoother the grind.)

Ollie onto the ledge and land with both trucks securely on the coping. **2**

3 Cruise along the coping.

When you feel yourself slowing down, shift your weight to the back, lift the nose, run, drop off, and roll away. **4**

5–0 GRIND

A 5–0 grind is like the 50–50 except that you only stick the back trucks, not both. Make sure you can do a 50–50 well before you try the 5–0.

1 Approach the object with some speed, at a 30-degree angle or less. Ollie as you would for a 50–50, but higher. You want to peak over the ledge, not on it.

Just before you peak, push your back foot down but leave your front foot at its original height (this angles the board backward).

2

3 As the back truck contacts the ledge, push down further. The wheels should be against the vertical part of the ledge.

Now balance in that position, grinding along until you drop off the end of the ledge or lose momentum and drop off the side.

4

PARK AND SKATE CAMP SESSIONS

Now you have the basics to skate and the beginning tricks to show your stuff. Skateparks have all the room and obstacles you can possibly need to practice and learn new tricks. If you have time in the summer, skateboarding camps offer day camps and overnight camps. Both give you all the time and instruction you can handle. Check out the camps listed in the For More Information section at the back of the book. Now get out there and tear it up!

Bellevue Skateboard Camp
14224 Bell Red Road
Bellevue, WA 98007
(425) 452-2722

Eisenberg's Summer Camp
Eisenberg's Skatepark
930 E. 15th Street
Plano, TX 75074
(972) 918-9593

Lake Owen Camp
HC 60 Box 60
Cable, WI 54821
(715) 798-3785

Mission Valley YMCA
5505 Friars Road
San Diego, CA 92110
(619) 298-3576

Skater Island Skate Camp
1747 W. Main Road
Middletown, RI 02842
(401) 848-8078

Woodward Camp
P.O. Box 93
134 Sports Camp Dr
Route 45
Woodward, PA 16882
(814) 349-5633

GLOSSARY

body varial To spin your body along its vertical axis (turning around) while the board does not spin.

bowl A vert or miniramp in a bowl shape.

burly A big trick that could hurt a lot if it isn't done right; also, a skater who prefers this type of trick.

bust A spot you are likely to get kicked out of; to bust a trick is also to perform it successfully (you are busting if you are skating well).

curb cut The transition between the bottom of a driveway and the top of a curb, used as a hip.

drop in To enter a ramp from the top platform.

flatbar z A rail or bar that is not sloped down stairs or an incline.

flat ground No obstacles, with the exception of something to trick over.

gap A distance between two riding surfaces that skaters ollie over (or do more advanced tricks over).

gnarly Amazing, radical.

halfpipe/vert ramp A ramp composed of a flat bottom with concave transition leading to vert on both sides.

handrail A rail that is down stairs or an embankment of moderate height.

hipper A large, painful strawberry bruise on the hip.

late trick Any trick that is executed after the board has reached its peak height in the air, or while airborne from another trick.

launch ramp A ramp used for launching a skater in the air.

line A number of tricks performed consecutively; path or planned course through a park or spot.

lock-in The act of getting your board into a very stable slide or grind position, so that you can slide or grind for a longer period of time.

manual A trick in which a skater balances his or her weight over the back truck, keeping the front wheels off of the ground.

mini ramp Like a halfpipe, but smaller, with mellower transition and no vert.

pump Flexing your legs at the right spot on a transition to build up speed.

quarterpipe or quarter A ramp with only one concave transition (two quarters facing each other would make up a vert or mini ramp, minus the connecting flatbottom).

ripper A really good and consistent skater

sketch or sketchy Used to describe an obstacle that isn't smooth or a trick that doesn't look easy; a person or situation that is fishy.

slam A hard fall.

slappie A grind on a ledge without ollieing.

slide Any trick in which any part of the deck is sliding atop an obstacle.

snake Someone who cuts you off or steals your line at a park or spot; also, to cut someone off or steal their line.

stall The act of getting your board into a sliding or grinding position on an obstacle, without sliding or grinding.

street skating Skating only with objects or obstacles found on the street.

transfer Whenever a skater transfers from one area to another; for example, from one ramp to another, approaching an obstacle from one side and riding away on the other side, and so on.

transition Any surface for skating that is not horizontal or vertical.

tweak To add style to a trick by exaggerating or contorting it.

FOR MORE INFORMATION

Skateparks

Here's a list of some public skateparks in the United States. Check out http://www.skatepark.org for more information, or to locate one closer to your own area.

Arvada Skatepark—A facility with one six-foot halfpipe, one four-foot halfpipe, an ollie box, a pyramid, and a bionic bow, located in Arvada, Colorado.

Campbell Skatepark—An outdoor skatepark with halfpipe and street course. Campbell, California.

Carson Warner Memorial Skatepark—An outdoor park with bowls and hips located in Healdsburg, California.

Cheapskates—Reading, Pennsylvania.

Chester Skatepark—Located in Chester, Vermont.

City of Claremont Skatepark—This skatepark is a 5,000-square-foot cement facility complete with two rails, one ledge, and a small cement bowl, located in Claremont, California.

Collier County Skatepark—A 20,000-square-foot street course complete with mini ramp located in Naples, Florida.

Columbia Skatepark—Located in Cosmo Park, Columbia, Missouri. This facility has an elaborate street course designed to entertain and challenge skaters.

Escondido Sports Center/Skatepark—An outdoor skatepark with vert ramp, street course, and mini ramp located in Escondido, California.

Exit 59 Skatepark—Cedar City, Utah.

FDR Skatepark—Philadelphia, Pennsylvania.

Graffiti Skate Zone—Located in Palm Bay, Florida.

Major Taylor Skatepark—Indianapolis, Indiana.

Millennium Skatepark—A large public skatepark in Calgary, Alberta, Canada.

Nav City Sk8 Park—A skateboard and inline skating park located right next to Navarre Beach Bridge, Navarre, Florida.

The Pipeline—An outdoor skatepark in Juneau, Alaska.

Provident Skatepark—Located in Visalia, California, for skates and skateboards.

Skateboarding, Rollerblading, Biking—Located in Woodbury, Connecticut.

Winslow, Arizona, Skatepark Project—Free, concrete skatepark. Located in Winslow, Arizona.

Web Sites

Due to the changing nature of Internet links, the Rosen Publishing Group, Inc., has developed an online list of Web sites related to the subject of this book. This site is updated regularly. Please use this link to access the list:

http://www.rosenlinks.com/ws/bgvc

FOR FURTHER READING

Brannon, Brian, and Kevin Thatcher.
  Thrasher: The Radical Skateboard Book. New York: Random
  House, 1992.
Brooke, Michael. *The Concrete Wave: The History of
  Skateboarding.* Toronto: Warwick Publishing, 1999.
Davis, James, and Skin Philips. *Skateboard Roadmap.* London:
  Carlton, 1999.
Gutman, Bill. *Skateboarding to the Extreme!* New York: St. Martin's
  Press, 1997.
Hawk,Tony, and Sean Mortimer. *Hawk: Occupation:
  Skateboarder.* New York: HarperCollins, 2000.

BIBLIOGRAPHY

Alberti, Elena. "Skateboarding Basics." Retrieved November 21, 2001 (http://www.nhsd.k12.pa.us/StudentWebpages/2001-02/albeele01).

"The Basics of Skateboarding" Retrieved November 21, 2001 (http://www.geocities.com/skater4100/basics1.html).

Brooke, Michael. *The Concrete Wave: The History of Skateboarding*. Toronto: Warwick Publishing, 1999.

Brooke, Michael. "A Short History of Skateboarding." Retrieved November 21, 2001 (http://www.recreate.com/Pages/articles/mbrooke.shtml).

Skateboard.com. "Skate101." Retrieved November 21, 2001 (http://www.skateboard.com/frontside/101/myride/assembly.asp).

"The Skateboarding Basics." Retrieved November 21, 2001 (http://www.geocities.com/jamen333/basics.html).

Skate Now! "Choosing-a-board." Retrieved November 21, 2001 (http://www.iprimus.ca/~gord/chooseboard.htm).

Skate Now! "Getting Started." Retrieved November 21, 2001 (http://www.globalserve.net/~gord/getstarted.htm).

INDEX

CREDITS

About the Author

Aaron Rosenberg was born in New Jersey, grew up in New Orleans, and now lives in New York. He has taught college English, worked in corporate graphics, and now runs his own game publishing company, Clockworks. He has written short stories, essays, poems, articles, novels, books, and role-playing games.

Acknowledgments

The editors would like to thank Sean McGuire at the Northridge Skatepark in Northridge, California, and Vic Vasquez from Val Surf in North Hollywood, California, for their time and cooperation.

Photo Credits

Cover, pp. 4, 6, 8, 13, 14, 15, 20, 22, 23, 25, 26, 27, 28, 29, 31, 32, 33, 34, 35, 37, 38 © Tony Donaldson/Icon SMI; p. 5 © Macduff Everton/Corbis; p. 12 © John-Marshall Mantel/Corbis.

Editors

Mark Beyer and Nicholas Croce

Design and Layout

Thomas Forget